Forget Me Nots

Carolina Freitas

Forget Me Nots © 2022 Carolina Freitas

All rights reserved.

No part of this publication may be reproduced, stored in a retrieval system, or transmitted, in any form or by any means, electronic, mechanical, photocopying, recording or otherwise, without the prior written permission of the presenters.

Carolina Freitas asserts the moral right to be identified as author of this work.

Presentation by *BookLeaf Publishing*

Web: www.bookleafpub.com

E-mail: info@bookleafpub.com

ISBN: 9789357690577

First edition 2022

To Sarah and Cierah

The industry: Part 1

Everywhere we turn
Supplements to lose weight
To build muscle
To tone
To erase belly fat
How are we supposed to love ourselves
In a world where we are bombarded with these
messages?
The industry profits from our self-hate

The industry: Part 2

I wish I could find the individuals who made it
normal for women to hate each other and ask
them if they are pleased with themselves

The Industry: Part 3

One day we will wake up
Reach our ideal weight
Fit into some arbitrary beauty standard
And feel the joy we are taught we are supposed
to feel
The lies we tell ourselves to avoid our feelings
We eat those too

The industry: Part 4

There are greed and profit in feeling shame and
self-hate
There are also pleasure and joy in realizing we
are not slaves to these industries

Power Struggle: Part 1

Happiness escapes me once in a while
I wish I could see it coming
I wish it gave me signs it was leaving
It catches me off guard
Forces me to push through the day, the week, the year
Not knowing when it will come back

Power Struggle: Part 2

I often feel like I'm drowning
Trying to come up for air
I want to let the waves take me
Off to another place
I can finally call home

Power Struggle: Part 3

I push myself when I'm on the edge
Then I'm surprised when I fall
It's no wonder why I feel frozen, stuck,
motionless
I'm hurt from the fall
Recovering from another injury

Power Struggle: Part 4

When I'm in unsteady waters
And I know I'll tip over soon
The suspense and the anguish are too much to
bear
Jumping in the turbulent ocean feels safer
Than waiting for the inevitable crash

Power Struggle: Part 5

I feel rushed even when I'm not
I fill my agenda with endless meaningless to-dos
I can't decide what to cross off
My body decides for me, wins the fight
And instead, it does nothing

The Parts of Me: Part 1

How come you come to see me out of nowhere?
No permission to enter
You ask your pointless questions
Refuse to hear reasonable answers
And leave me with so many more doubts than I
started with
Only to resurface again without any invitation

The Parts of Me: Part 2

Your presence is loud and clear
You don't have to stomp so loud my dear
Like a toddler who needs attention
You don't stop
I hear, see, and feel you
When you make me act in ways that don't make
sense
When you make my heart race
Wanting attention
Making me stop for air to breath

The Parts of Me: Part 3

I would like to know when it stops
When I can stop trying new methods to keep you
away
When I can live in peace and contemplate life
and all its wonders
When can I accept you and let you go?
When can you accept me and let me go?

The Parts of Me: Part 4

Do I befriend you and show compassion and
grace?
Do I treat you like a bully, like evil who tortures
me?
Do I accept you and observe from a distance?
I don't understand why you continue to stay
after all I've done to let you go

Disconnection: Part 1

I feel so lost
I see faces and smiles
All I hear is gibberish
Not knowing what is real or imagined
I go through the motions of life
Wondering when I will finally have a
breakthrough
When life will start to make sense

Disconnection: Part 2

15

When will I wake up from this trance, this
dream, this hypnotic state that is supposed to be
life?

Disconnection: Part 3

I wish the world stopped
So I could get off
Go to another planet
Since this one feels foreign to me
Maybe I'm not meant for planet earth

Disconnection: Part 4

It still feels like a bad dream, a horrible movie
with a plotline full of holes
It doesn't make sense
Makes me question reality
It's inconsistent, has no logic
When reality hits
I hope I don't fall apart

Connection: Part 1

I long for a day
Where I do nothing
Where I talk to no one
Where I lay down and contemplate life

Connection: Part 2

It's easy to get angry at the wrong thing, the
wrong person, the wrong moment
So hold on to your anger
Listen to it closely
It will tell you stories
That you need to understand to let it go

Connection: Part 3

Sometimes we think we are alone in universal
feelings
In sadness, happiness, shame, guilt, joy, despair,
anger
We all experience these feelings together and
apart
That's the irony of it all

Connection: Part 4

Somewhere out there, a person is struggling
Be kind, be present, be attentive
You don't know how many of you are out there

www.ingramcontent.com/pod-product-compliance
Lightning Source LLC
LaVergne TN
LVHW050306200726
843509LV00015B/3183